MUSEUM OF ICE CREAM

Jenna Clake was born in Staffordshire in 1992. Her debut collection of poetry, *Fortune Cookie*, won the Melita Hume Prize in 2016, and was published in 2017 by Eyewear. It received an Eric Gregory Award from the Society of Authors in 2018, and was shortlisted for a Somerset Maugham Award in the same year. Her pamphlet of prose poems, *CLAKE/ Interview for*, was published by Verve Poetry Press in 2018, and was featured as a spring pamphlet in the Poetry Book Society Bulletin in 2019. She was shortlisted for the inaugural Rebecca Swift Women Poets' Prize, commended in the University of Hertfordshire Single Poem Prize, and placed second in the Newcastle Poetry Prize in 2018. Her second full collection, *Museum of Ice Cream*, was published by Bloodaxe Books in 2021. She lectures at Teesside University.

JENNA CLAKE

Museum
of Ice Cream

BLOODAXE BOOKS

ISBN: 978 1 78037 545 8

First published 2021 by
Bloodaxe Books Ltd,
Eastburn,
South Park,
Hexham,
Northumberland NE46 1BS.

www.bloodaxebooks.com
For further information about Bloodaxe titles
please visit our website and join our mailing list
or write to the above address for a catalogue

Supported using public funding by
**ARTS COUNCIL
ENGLAND**

Cover design: Neil Astley & Pamela Robertson-Pearce.

Printed in Great Britain by Bell & Bain Limited, Glasgow, Scotland, on
acid-free paper sourced from mills with FSC chain of custody certification.

ACKNOWLEDGEMENTS

Thank you to the editors of the publications in which some of these poems, or earlier versions, appeared: *The Poetry Review, The White Review, The Rialto, Oxford Poetry, The Stinging Fly, The Tangerine, Minola Review, Magma, Bath Magg, The Valley Press Anthology of British Prose Poetry, Islands Are But Mountains: New poetry from the United Kingdom.*

'Tell me if you prefer your carrots as sticks or coins and I'll always remember' was highly commended in the University of Hertfordshire Single Poem Prize. 'I try to make sense of things by standing very close to windows' was placed second in the Newcastle Poetry Competition. 'Wooden doll, total being' won the BareFiction poetry prize. Thank you to the judges.

With love and thanks to: my family, Luke, Izzy, Cynthia, Miles, Richard, Millie, Elisha, Jane.

Several of these poems were first written during my PhD at the University of Birmingham. Thank you to the Creative Writing department, and the College of Arts and Law for the resources and funding to write these and many other poems. I'm grateful to Jack Underwood, Ruth Gilligan, and Elsa Braekkan Payne for their insight.

With thanks to Matthew Turner and Neil Astley.

CONTENTS

Cloud Appreciation Society

Then came the day that we saw a cloud attached to a parachute,
heading down towards us...

We caught the cloud lovingly,
and asked if it wanted to stay with us...

It asked to keep the parachute on, and we let it...

And we took the cloud to bed with us, one by one,
not to sleep with it, but next to it...

We felt so wonderful with our arms wrapped around the cloud...

When it slept, it breathed like the sound inside a shell...

We were jealous when it slept
next to someone else...

We asked it to stay, and held it too tightly...

Before it left, it told us it would be back soon, but that it was a cloud,
and part of being a cloud was needing to move around...

We would have to open the window wide for it,
let it squeeze past us to get out...

We would watch it push itself into the sky
and parachute into the next house...

We felt a heavy rain in our stomachs...

I would die for you in the best way possible

As soon as you walked up to each other, you knew
the bench in a snowstorm was edible. One of you felt
like a shark egg, the other felt like I do
constantly: stepping on a just-mopped floor.
You listened to each other breathing as you walked
up the stairs, lungs like twisted straws:
one of you struggling, and the other steady
as the floor levelled. I looked at girls with fried eggs
printed on their skirts, tried to remember the face
of someone who told me they liked my t-shirt,
went back to the café eight months later in hope
of finding them. One of you felt cellulite through
your leggings, the other felt like I do sometimes:
ashamed when the microwave stops.
You thought about how things might have been
different, like candle pin being the most popular
form of bowling; if only the goggles had been red;
if only you didn't mind being seen together,
pink tiles in a light green bathroom.

Wooden doll, total being

They were always saying that I had my father's nose or my father's eyebrows or my father's ears until I saw my body like a wooden doll's: hanging together delicately, easily ripped apart. To argue, my parents went outside and stood around the corner of the house by the shed. There were marks where my father had kicked the wall. Suppose he was trying to get out, rather than in? I wanted an argument but there was no one to argue with. Went to the wall and kicked it, left marks over my father's. I had his legs now too, or his feet. Whichever they said. I lay at the top of the stairs like a cat bored of chasing. Tried to pull my nose off with my fingers. Then they said I had my father's hands, so what was I supposed to do? My mother came into my bedroom at night and touched my nose, eyebrows and ears and said, 'How can you be upset to look like this?' She walked around in her underwear, all the slim, calm folds of her. There were mirrors everywhere and they felt cool against my skin.

Immersive experience of all the things I want (that are bad for me)

On the perfect TV date, we go to the fun fair, eat candy floss
as light as a tutu skirt. My teeth are still white
and smooth like a bathtub. We play mini golf –
I lose – and we get burgers; none of the lettuce
falls out, our fries are perfectly straight.

Or we go to an art gallery with interactive,
walk-through exhibitions, and I hit my head
on entering one. When I tell my sister,
she says, he must really like you, then, having
seen you do that, and so I don't mention
that I didn't say that I was starving the whole time.

*In this simulation you are the lime green fan
in the corner of the room. There is a glass of ice
and water in front of you. This is the only object
available to help you alert people to your presence,
to the fact that you are trapped inside the fan.*

Vixen

when I was in primary school one of my classmates believed he was in love with me once a week he would leave little presents and love letters in my tray the notes would say things like I think you are really pretty and would end in a thousand kisses there was a teacher who used to fill pupils' trays with water and then scream at them to get something out of them so that one or two children would be soaked as they rushed to get their exercise books when I opened my tray there would be an envelope covered in flowers or paper butterflies covered in glitter they were always the purple of my favourite grape-scented gel pen and I never told anyone that the grape was my favourite which meant he was watching me friends would gather around me and say has he done it again? we'd try to hide it from the teacher and then throw it unopened into a bin because we knew that we'd be the ones to get in trouble if it was discovered I was always wiping my hands down the front of my jumper like there was something on them he hid one in my school bag I was the last to leave at the end of the day I thought I could throw it into the bin without anyone seeing my teacher had followed me out of the room and for some reason looked into the bin in the cloakroom where the letter sat on top with my name on the front he held it out to me like I should have been pleased about it

How much longer until I get this out?

You are eating fig rolls
because your mother thinks
you like them, as she does,
and she wraps them in paper
napkins like slices of cake;
you found the fig rolls
in the pocket of your bag,
and you want her to keep on
buying them so you are never
able to tell the truth,
so that you eat them until
they remind you of her
and you have grown
to like them like you taught
a boyfriend to like olives and
then to like mushrooms,
as though this were improving
him as a person, but really
he was lactose intolerant,
as was the other woman he was fucking.

I wanted Agent Cooper to save my life

When the door opened it was Agent Cooper
He came and sat at my table   He said
something about dead pies   and I said Do you
know that is my favourite line   He was
smoothing the plastic tablecloth with his hands
I had never wanted a massage more   He said
You know we had to throw up all those
doughnuts after we ate them and I said Oh don't
tell me that but it was too late and I opened my
eyes in the darkness and I swung my feet to the
floor   Where are you going said my
boyfriend   I said I have to get these doughnuts
out of me   He rolled towards me and touched
my back   He said I can't remember anything
from the beginning of us   I rubbed my
collar bone as I always did

In this simulation a ginger cat sleeps
on your navy blue desk chair.
When you try to pick him up,
he digs his claws into the seat, tearing it.
You make low, soothing sounds.

Sponge cake, pound cake, gateau

I   never   meant to   write   a list of the places I have cried   but
I do recommend it   as a therapeutic act   once I cried in a
department store   while shopping for the perfect fudge   but
maybe you've done it too   my lemon mousse   my blueberry
genoese   I also cried in the bathroom   of a very nice
gin bar   I overheard someone I loved   make a cruel joke
at my expense   my coffee cake   my pistachio slice   it
is sad to know   that too many desserts   are disappointing
why couldn't I get a raspberry tart   instead of a strawberry one
my banoffee pie   my star-shaped shortbread   every
day   I ask the world   for what I   want   my champagne
macaron   my chocolate meringue   what if a joke isn't a
joke   but a slow destruction   my gin cocktail   came
with   jelly babies   and I didn't even   eat them

there is no marine snow here, my friend

out of the cereal box came an eel
and the eel only came out because
i had tipped the contents of the cereal
box onto the kitchen floor

wasn't there meant to be a plastic bag
inside and do you remember how
at one point the bags were foil
and we were promised freshness
like how everyone seems to want
me and my body

the eel was curling back on itself like a pretzel
we are all searching for something edible
i said out loud like it would be a comfort
even though i knew it couldn't be

eventually the eel stopped twisting
and i stepped on the cereal box
what a morning for an incredible graveyard

Self-portrait as the opening of a window on a hot morning

Three men carry a large snake home between them. This morning, the pantry was empty again, the sun in the sky like a lemon slice. They daydream of fried potatoes, mayonnaise like sun-cream. The youngest of the men, a boy, asks the oldest of the men, his father, to describe the following items: walnut, peach, salt, goat's cheese, apple. The father says, 'Tremendous loss! Tremendous chaos! Tremendous emptiness! Tremendous cracker! Tremendous yellow!' and thinks of a woman who always slept on the sofa as he cleaned her windows. Her legs like caramel from a tin, another life. The other man, also a boy, the eldest boy, and also the son of the father, looks at people in the park, all in pairs or groups. There is a wedding party. He sees the bride's head over the rows of anemones, violas and benches, her hair like a stick of liquorice. He thinks of how he has a particular tree to sit under, how he has spent whole days under there. If he sits alone all day and talks to no one, does he exist? Sometimes he scavenges change to buy a bottle of water, just to have spoken. Later, as his parents cut the snake into rations, as he spins the snake's skull around his finger, his mother asks if he wants something to drink, and he believes he has responded. When he sees the steam rising from their mugs of broth, he accuses her of forgetting him, goes outside, walks to the river and unsticks a limpet.

Organisational Skills for the Hungry

I couldn't get out of bed because I was disorganised
This is what they told me
If you're disorganised you can't be happy
The sheets fell on top of me and were weighed down with sand
The sand was in the bed but I couldn't see it

I'm hungry but don't know what to eat
My stomach tells me this daily
I try to say it is past midday and this makes me afraid
How will I make it

~

I was disorganised so they bought me a calendar
I was told to fill the days with walking and praying
On the first day I wrote breakfast lunch dinner
I was tired from the effort
I ran my hand over the words and smudged them

This was my greatest victory

~

When I eat everything sticks to my teeth
I'm constantly brushing them
I lie on the bed and let the sun hit me
It's the only way to feel pure

The best way to fill a day is to colour it
I painted each day white with Tipp-Ex
Good days are blue
Everything beautiful is blue

~

Everywhere people are listing the things they eat
This is exactly what I'm not supposed to do

I reached down inside me and held the rumbling tight
I reached down inside me and rocked it back to sleep

~

They told me to write a poem about it
I showed them the white calendar
They said it was the wrong kind of poem

When I eat everything gets all over my face
I coloured the lids of peanut butter jars white
They said I should be ashamed of myself

I told them there is no room for anything else

In this simulation you realise you're becoming
a woman when you hear the boys' deeper voices.
You sleep on your front to stop your body growing.

Milk, Strawberry, Sugar

My first thought after every meal is: there's no one
to tell me when I have something stuck in my teeth,
so I dream of a man serving ice cream with a large
silver spoon. He ladles the ice cream onto my hot, naked
body and then licks it off with dedication and worship.
This all takes place in a neon-lit dessert bar,
where something violent is about to happen.

The omission is meaningless

Here is what happened: a daughter tried to please her parents. She tried to stop eating and dedicated it to her family. The daughter got a sliver of apple stuck between her front teeth and dedicated it to her shame. The daughter's sister became pregnant and gave their mother everything she had ever wanted. The daughter felt hot shame rising through her body and cold shame sinking to her feet, like wet sand had got stuck in her shorts and was heavily falling out. The daughter got a boyfriend. The daughter and the boyfriend went to the beach. The daughter asked the boyfriend to write something in the sand for her. The sea was suddenly full of boats; the beach was full of stray dogs. The boyfriend wrote *send shells*, then went swimming and didn't return. The daughter dedicated this to her family. The daughter went walking and it rained from the moment she left to the moment she got home. The daughter shaved her legs obsessively and ran a finger over the blades to see how many times she could avoid being cut. She dedicated this to her father, who had always wanted sons.

M's letters to tumblr

1

I called my parents and said 'I think I have a problem' I eat until I get to the bottom of the cereal box which is my favourite part I mix the dust of cornflakes with milk to make a paste my stomach gets round like something is growing inside it

Once a week I walk five minutes to the local Tesco to fill a basket I go up to my bedroom eat as much as possible then put the rest on the kitchen table 'I bought all of this and I don't know why' I say to my housemates and they say 'if you're sure?' and then I go back upstairs again

N made 100 lemon and orange shortbread biscuits to last all eight of us until we go home for break N baked everything but I helped ice them we began intricately then eventually drizzled the icing over the biscuits until they looked like mirrors splashed with toothpaste 'I'm so tired of doing this' said N and I knew exactly how she felt

My parents were out with friends they said they'd call me back later or the next morning but it has been three mornings and I'm not sure how long later is

2

Last night I cleaned almost every room in this three-storey house and this morning it is filthy again I had to sweep hair shavings into the sink and I cried when my housemates saw they told me I was over-bearing so I bought six peanut butter KitKats and put them in a line on the kitchen surface and wrote 'I'm sorry' on a scrap of paper

There are five magpies in the garden and they sit on the fire escape outside my bedroom window and wake me up early every morning tomorrow I am asking them to come earlier so that they can kill me faster than this other thing will

Of the 100 biscuits N made I have eaten fifty N is commenting on how quickly our house eats the things she bakes and is knocking on our doors to ask how many we have eaten I pretend to not be in my room and sneak out only to go to the bathroom

3

I wish you would reply to me I particularly like the way you take photos everything is always so colourful my one housemate T only eats green things and laughs at how beige I am but is always taking snacks out of my fridge

Yes I was in love a year or so ago but life goes on they say being in love is like your favourite book cover being made into a cake and not being in love is crying when the Tesco cashier calls you brave I am trying a new flavour of noodles today and yes that is brave

T is always going to the gym and we are meant to say things like 'I wish I had your motivation' and 'wow you look great' but people are always saying things to me that they shouldn't N tells me that I eat a lot and my mother tells me I eat like a bird the magpies outside my window never eat so perhaps my mother is a liar

Here are three things no one knows about me and I'm going to list them one is that my favourite sweets are Parma Violets two is that I can't eat them any more and three is that I don't mind it when there's no hot water left and my body has to work harder to stay warm

4

A woman cried so much she had no water left in her and when she tried to drink she felt it going down then pouring out of a hole under her ribs she was always cold friends would tell her they had seen her old boyfriend and she wanted to tell them to stop but instead nodded and asked questions

The woman sat in a very deep bath and tried to poke water into the hole under her ribs but of course water doesn't go that way and she sat in there until she was very wrinkled and her skin looked like it was melting and then it did

She was part of the water and liked the silence of it she travelled around as water for a while and felt what it was like to give life to something like a fish or coral she didn't feel the need to cry any more

5

I fell out with N or rather N fell out with me I was too weak to go to L's birthday party I sat at the kitchen table with my head in my hands and N said 'we all feel tired' and slammed a cupboard door which was very similar to the way she slammed my bedroom door when I admitted to eating all the biscuits I offered to bake some more I'm actually quite good at it but N had eaten a dinner of just eggs and beans and I think she was trying to prove a point Every time I go shopping I buy two jars of peanut butter the public one which is crunchy and I eat with crackers and the private one which is smooth and I eat from the jar with my hands today I fell over in the shower and couldn't get up later A said he heard me and wondered what it was

I saw a man in a black sports car the roof was down and he was holding onto the steering wheel with one hand and with the other was holding a banana I think I laughed when I got back I was shivering N said 'you're always so cold what is that a vitamin thing?'

6

Sometimes I imagine you are here too we'll sit in the shade in the park our pins and needles will be so bad when we stand up we will laugh until we can walk another friend will get engaged and sit cross-legged on the floor to tell us and another friend will create an ethical mobile phone company from his bedroom and another friend will wear shorts exclusively and we will laugh at his very pale legs I think I always want a different thing like eating a curry with a spoon or chopsticks N won't stop telling me every time she skips lunch or dinner she has a very empty cupboard and I'm not sure which of us I want to be

When we leave this place we'll be real friends and maybe won't have to leave post-it notes on our butter I admit that I have been stealing A's cheese my mother visited today and saw my rotten bag of spinach and handed me £20

When we were younger my parents made my sister and I finish our vegetables before we left the table if it was peas we would chew slowly then open our mouths at each other to see what a mess we'd made

Like other women

you might come out of your house dressed as a clown
and meet another girl your age, dressed as a clown; as you might
go to the cinema together, dressed as clowns, and not eat
popcorn; as you might, wearing your clown costumes underneath,
try on new clothes and point out to each other where the clown
suit is showing; as you might go to a restaurant and ask for two
empty plates, and roll your red noses around them; as you might,
sitting in her bedroom as she is in the bathroom, find a drawer
filled with eggs and oranges; as you might, whilst throwing up
in the bathroom, worry about her finding your drawer filled
with chocolate; as you might send emails to keep each other
on track; as you might direct each other to websites
about how to be better clowns; as you might stop talking
to your other friends in order to spend more time with her;
as you both might wake up early to go for a run dressed as clowns; as
you might want to take off your clown suit, but know
that you need the other one to undo the zip; as you might
hug each other at the end of the day, and at the same time check
that the other one is still wearing all the parts of her costume.

I hid fish in my pockets and forgot about it for days

After Jane Wong

Anything that is not a vegetable is evil.

When we eat, our souls become heavier, like wet flour.

I splatter tomato juice up the tiles on purpose; I am dangerous.

Ceremony is another word for obsession.

I am honest enough to realise that.

To see success, look at the glassiness of eyes in photographs.

To see failure, well, you know what to do.

How terrible to feel locked out of life, to not know the secret.

My mother calls to tell me the bad news she has been hiding.

She taps the phone anxiously; you suffer so much already.

Remember: you're not as good at hiding things as you think you are.

Siesta for Olivia

My parents took me on holiday and when we got to the beach a girl from my dance class was there. We were best friends for two weeks; we climbed the rocks and watched people dive into the sea. The sea was the blue of a brand new pen. I would only eat chips with ketchup for dinner. Someone put squid on my plate and I screamed. A cockroach was squashed with a milk carton. It's possible to say that the holiday where the pizza got covered in flies was the start of all the trouble; when I got home I realised that the scariest thing about everything is knowing it can't last, like a box of cereal, or a bag of crisps, or willpower.

In this simulation you have been told
to leave your house within the hour.
Someone is knocking on the front door.
With your mother, you are gently stacking
plates on the steps of the swimming pool.

All our problems began with a woman eating

I saw a man walking
across a bridge with a tray of lemons,
each one perfectly lined up
and cradled by its lemon sisters.
I could love you! I thought
as the tray went past, but honestly
I don't know if I meant to say it
to the man or the lemons.

On feeling my eggshell heart break

I put my ear to a mug of green tea and heard the ocean;
my best friend hunched over as she rode her bike to work.
She came over later with a majestic pasta bake. I borrowed
her bike and rode it for twenty-four hours in a very large circle
until there was no more pasta. I had cycled past the sea
and thought about going in, but I put my ear to the handlebars
and heard a meadow. When I got to the meadow, it said,
Why do something when the world could do it for you?
I said, *The world can't do anything, because I don't know how to ask.*
I forgave the meadow for not knowing about my eggshell heart,
but to teach it a lesson I took off my shoes and walked all over it.
I cycled back to my best friend, chewing on the head of a pretty, pretty pansy.

Jen's Sweet Shop

when I go shopping   with my friends   we wait for the
animatronic unicorn   to move   just a   little nod   to let
us know   its spirit   hasn't died   there are   five
different types   of unicorn   and we rank them   from
best   to   worst   the little round unicorns   with big round
eyes   are my least favourite   and somewhere   a child
is crying   curled   like an empty   white bowl   having put
the wrong sweets   into her   pick n mix bag   and
knowing it   and really   an animatronic   unicorn   is
a good way   to describe   how I feel about my   body
and how I feel   when someone   tells me   my choices
are unhealthy   the way I   move   slightly   and   someone
does a   double-take   to   make sure   I am real

In this simulation you block the toilets
in your office building by trying to flush
chocolate bar wrappers;
they unfurl like fortune-telling fish.

i am driving for hours tonight; i didn't bring snacks

learning to drive i wouldn't see myself
    on an evening walk i'm as wild as i can get
in the car alone
    griping like a little yappy dog
visiting the doctor about my iron levels
    imagining myself running into my sister in the supermarket
instructing me on the bread and butter instead
    tiger loaf and chicken in her basket
telling me to be shrill at a different time of day
    identifying the permeability of my two worlds
ignoring the pamphlet i'm meant to pick up from reception
    the world i have and the one with everyone else in it
squashing red berries on my evening walk
    will i ever want to make a sandwich again
getting annoyed with myself for tramping them into the carpet

I could cry, yes, I could

Unpeeling a clementine or a sweet wrapper,
stuffing my hand in a cookie jar,
squashing little red bugs on the shower wall,
picking at the plaster, thinking about licking my thumb.

Out the window there are pale red
maybe purple hills saying this could
have all kinds of repercussions for your body
you don't want that to happen, do you?

It's no longer about us, it's got to be about me
After The O.C.

What if my life is a film where I'm a teenage girl and I'm dating an older man... say like seventeen and twenty-eight... and my parents are aware... and I have an internet stalker but I've been ignoring him... and I'm American and white...we all are... and I'm in the car with my mother and younger brother... say like forty and fourteen... and I'm driving the black range rover I was given for my sixteenth birthday... and every time my stomach growls I turn the radio up... and the radio happens to be playing mine and my boyfriend's song... and my mother says, Honey are you happy?... and I say, I'm really happy I love our song... and my mother says, What is it?... and I'm wearing this headband that has panda ears attached to it so I look like a panda... and it keeps slipping down so I keep on pushing it up... and I ask my mother to check the traffic to see if I can turn at a junction... and my brother is texting silently in the back... and he says, Can we go to McDonald's?... and I say, Sure... and at the Drive-thru he gets a burger, some fries and a milkshake... and my mother asks for napkins and a doughnut... and I get nothing... and five minutes later my brother says, I'm still hungry I should've got the apple pie... and at the same time my internet stalker arrives at my older boyfriend's house... and my boyfriend lets him in because he thinks the stalker is my friend... and my stalker is wearing a black hoodie and panda ears like mine... and when my boyfriend has let him in my stalker says, I am here to kidnap you... and my boyfriend says, Why?... and then my stalker says that he loves me... and uses my name which is something cool and American like Avery or Aubrey... and my boyfriend and my stalker argue... and my stalker says, Why did you let me in?... and my boyfriend says he thought my stalker was another friend of mine... and he uses their name which is also something cool and American like Jackson or Brandon... and my stalker says, Jackson? or Brandon? our body types are totally different... and I'm still driving in the car with my mother and brother... and it's not clear where we're going... and I ask my brother to open the window to get rid of the smell of burger... and my phone keeps on going off... and because I'm in America I can answer it so I do... and it's my internet stalker calling but he has one of those voice-changers... and he says, If you ever want to see your boyfriend again you need to bring me ten unmelted ice creams in the next hour... and I definitely know where to find him even though he hasn't given me his location... and I do a u-turn in the middle of traffic... and no one gets hurt... and I'm wearing a very cute top and some shorts... and the outfit shows off my fragile frame... and it's not unusual because every girl I know has a body like mine... and at the same time my boyfriend wakes up and my internet stalker has tied him to the bed by his ankle... and as my boyfriend comes round he realises he is not in his own bedroom... and he starts shouting my name... and pulling at the ankle strap... and I've got the ten ice creams... and my mother is holding them in her lap... and she's telling me the quickest way to my stalker's location which is obviously the beach... and the ice cream is beginning to run down the side of the cones... and my brother is doing some internet research... and has figured out who my stalker is... and we are all shocked... and we've got one ice cream of each flavour because it's so much better visually... and as I'm driving I think for a moment about pulling over... and eating all the ice creams... and letting my stomach be quiet for a while... and then I realise I can't ruin the moment where my mother finally accepts my boyfriend... and convinces my father that he's actually alright... and where my brother and I will finally get one another... so I keep on driving...

Elegy for Balto from the Bottom of a Frozen Lake

and later we all fell down with a sickness and the antitoxin was 600 miles away if you are a wolf-dog then I am walking along aisles of chocolate bars picking them up and putting them straight down I believe my body should fit behind a face cloth and that is why I'd make a terrible parent if you are a bear fight then I am willing to lose and limp home without you tell me how a dog's face is prettier than mine if you are a dusty piano then I am false markers on the route back if you are light refracted through a broken glass jar then I am a deep growling an injured paw an uncredited snow goose racing to beat you and never quite making it

In this simulation, you watch a documentary
with your father about people like you.
He says, 'All these people are mad,'
which you guess is strictly correct.

Quayside of Dogs

now that I've cut my finger three times   I really hate mushrooms
a knife is like a vegetarian buffet   where only one thing is
vegetarian   or a promenade populated with exotic breeds of
dog   on holiday I ate   two chocolate eclairs a day   in the
orangery   there were no oranges   and oh! sometimes I make
little whimpering sounds   when no one is around   I conducted
an experiment to see   if a mushroom could go mouldy because
technically   a mushroom is already mould   it went mouldy
but you already knew that   I like crying   in multi-storey car parks
and checking the menu   before I go to eat   pretending
I've never seen it   on the promenade the dogs   are
always waiting   they are fabulous well-groomed demons and oh!
sometimes   the whimpers   become a voice saying   do you
wish   you were dead   and I say   yes   did you know
you can   boil   an egg   until it burns   and then   pops

Self-portrait as a pink dressing room

Crack an egg in half and see
how a person always
has a story about finding
a chick inside the shell,
and then you'd dream of
this person doing the saddest thing:
making their own birthday cake.
They would pick two flavours
that reminded them of someone,
strawberry and rhubarb, forgetting
that one will overpower
the other. Sadder still,
to put some in your mouth
and find it has gone sour.
Imagine everyone decided
to wear the blue of a J-Cloth
on the same day, but you wore pink.
I leave flour on my clothes so
it looks like I've been touched.

In this simulation, you go to a local bakery
and buy everything from the discounted
items shelf. When you get home,
you put two things on each plate,
making sure they don't touch.

Bread, orange, aura

She went to a camp where the coach was so angry she didn't feed them breakfast, or the coach was so angry she made a pot of tea and a bowl of bread and put them in the middle of the table, and they were scared of her, so didn't touch anything. She went to a school where they exercised in the morning before lessons. They would stand in a field in rows and stretch their fingers and their necks. Their backs would be stretched on Wednesdays. They all wore orange tracksuits. Some mornings the fog would be so thick that it cut people in half and fifty-one percent of the world would go missing. Sometimes she would be put in touch with distant relatives who didn't respond to her earnest emails. Sometimes she would challenge herself to not eat lunch, especially when the coach had refused to give them breakfast. She went to a school where ten percent of her marks were based on her aura. Her aura was the feeling of returning to primary school and being too big for the chairs. Some weekends she went home on the train with her friends. They hunched over their phones trying to complete calculations the fastest, talked about what the bread would taste like if they dared.

Oyster Delight

on days when the dirt gets in my eyes I hide in the back of an ice
cream van I know this is the last place you think I'd be but the
embrace of the inside of a chest freezer is everything I need if you
toss and turn on the wrappers of ice creams you can hear the sea
once I was lying in there and a bead of sweat ran from my armpit
to my elbow then I really knew that I was alive yes I have shaved
my legs using soft serve and yes I have passed the time building
towers from chocolate flakes peering out the window at the road
and snapping it shut when someone wants something from me
seeing how long I can keep my hand between the magnums before
it goes numb playing the ice cream van music and singing along
sometimes I think there is a secret code between ice cream vans
and what happens if I don't know the distress signal what if I
need someone to run to me like they've just been given pocket
money I feel calmer when I am listening to the insides of the
oyster shell wafers or writing my name in chocolate sauce I have
discovered that an overripe strawberry makes an excellent lipstick

In this simulation you paint a fish skeleton
onto the bottom of a cereal bowl.
Aware that someone is trying to take your photo,
you pull your hair over your face.

if you're near the park, come find me, i'm having a picnic

in the hotel i took all the remaining
tea bags the chocolates left for the pillows
also one individually wrapped
chocolate & hazelnut pastry from the buffet
& the needle from the sewing kit

i spooned the cold parts
of the scrambled eggs onto my plate
& let them melt on my tongue
no one there knew if i wore
the same outfit two days in a row
or ate a box of crackers
for dinner lying on the bed

i called the reception desk
as i was talking to the receptionist
i could hear them eating &
i was reminded that this whole thing
could have been a sundae drizzled in sunshine

& also that every time i use chopsticks
i feel like i'm on a third date
a split second from placing them down
on a napkin & reaching for the sushi
with my hands

Still life of newspapers folded on a bistro set

I was trying to get to something laeotropic when I threw the sun-dried sheets over my head and ate a balcony breakfast, granola falling off the spoon. There had better be Viennese whirls in the cut glass jar I said even though the jar was really a rose bowl. I was made to calculate a measurement using a chart. I was told to stop having so much cheese and butter and white bread, but I lied on the test and after that it was easy to lie some more, the sheets slowly torn apart, pulled over the railings. I wanted to record my friend's heartbeat and when I couldn't find it I was accused of touching her inappropriately, the twist of a cinnamon pastry. It is impossible to feel like a Campari evening on a winter beach, a slice of sweet potato falling out the spiraliser, when what I asked for was a bar of white chocolate.

Sunday roast on a dark wood table

After Gertrude Stein

In the inside there is eating, in the outside there is too much
lemon, whole wedges in the casserole, walnuts on their own.
In their own beautiful corners with green and gold glass, forgetting
to bring lunch, chilled butter with dusty green furniture, a sleeve turned
grey from wiping the top of a mirror. In raincoat pockets filled
with shells my mother is slicing a joint of beef with an electric
carving knife, feet in a cold swimming pool, tennis courts lined
with blossom. In the violent luck of this life, I bite into a boiled egg
like an apple; I'm not saying it wouldn't be better with custard.

In this simulation you are served
ice cream in a pink paper cup
with a wooden spoon. The ice cream
is bland. You hold the cup up to a
white wall, take a photograph.

I try to make sense of things by standing very close to windows

I

Morning felt like an ungraceful
attempt to pull myself
onto the side of a swimming pool

II

I wanted to dream of sash windows,
iced coffee mixing with milk / a yellow cup
and buttercream, the cold air hitting
the room kindly

III

I was asked to draw around
my silhouette in profile / I was shocked
and frightened by the shape of my nose

IV

I wondered how to make
my life better and concluded that all
I needed was a white apartment
and a couple of chairs, three slices
of quiche / a lily pad of desire

V

It was too cold to go in the sea
but too warm to wear a coat

VI

I touched white scarves
until I became vanilla

VII

Like seagulls roosting
on thin ledges, bridges,
everyone was pregnant or dying
or wrongly visiting a deli counter
looking for the perfect peach

VIII

I took a photo of my silhouette / it was a friend
covering their face with an umbrella,
blue and white striped curtains
knocking over a vase / a woman leaving
the pharmacy crying

IX

I tapped the powder from a custard
doughnut onto a plate,
it was like being given permission
to grow my body hair / it had something to do with respect

Tell me if you prefer your carrots as sticks or coins and I'll always remember

The last carrot you pull will always be the best, someone once said, but you can think of carrots as torches – eat them and you can stay up all night playing with a labrador. You might cook a carrot in honey and butter but you can just as easily chew until you can't swallow, or find it in your potato in lumps. A labrador's eyes are sprouts in torchlight, its wet, slobbery tongue a small fork, the head of a cauliflower, or a rabbit from one of the fields. A rabbit might prefer cabbage but a sundial can tell you when it is time to be hungry, hungrier and hungriest, or be garden gloves, ones too short to protect you from nettles, or a cat on the roof of the shed. A labrador might wait for you in the pagoda but you can always throw a basketball over the fence with a shovel. A smaller dog might crawl under the fence and bark to be let out, but you can't run full speed in wellington boots. It might be quiet enough to hear the slugs eating strawberry leaves, but you can't always hear a hand being accidentally placed on a still-hot hob, or tools falling from their hooks, or a cat asking to be rescued from behind the shed. The raspberries might be ripe, they said, and they might be your favourite fruit, they said, but a labrador will always guard the back door and follow you out in the morning.

Garments I have dreamed of but will never wear

A beige mackintosh hanging on the back of the door –
I am waiting for the person; the peeling
of a squash or the folds of their dark green scarf;
squares of light on the wall, or the person tucking in
the label sticking out the back of my dress,
a lemon-shaped trinket dish, or an enamel pot for tea;
oysters cracked open on an unmade bed of noodles:
the feeling that I am doing something very, very wrong
with the person; then the person's jumper with fluff
of a dandelion, and figs sliced open – inner-lip pink;
or I am standing at a pedestrian crossing looking up
at the person, wanting to touch their sleeve; or the person
turns to me as I am driving, listening to what I say.

In this simulation you are in a fitting room,
trying on clothes. In the angled mirror
behind you, you can see lines of bruises
down either side of your spine. Your hair
is so short now, you can't smell it.